AF302981

THE UNIVERSAL DECLARATION OF HUMAN RIGHTS

The Fight for Fundamental Freedoms

Written by Romain Parmentier
Translated by Jessica Foster

History 50MINUTES.com

50MINUTES.com

BECOME AN EXPERT
IN HISTORY

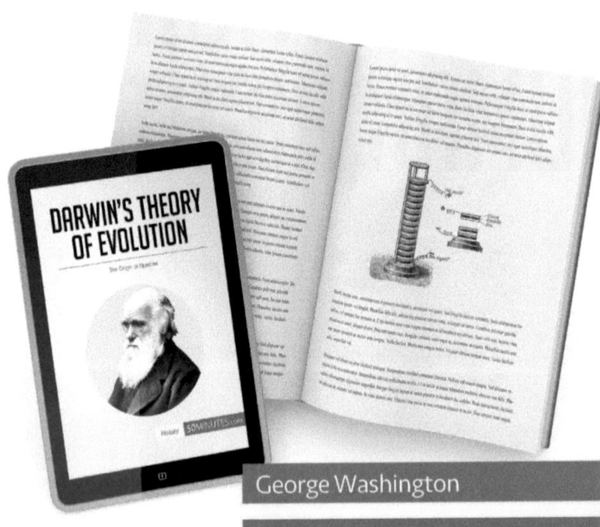

George Washington

The Battle of Austerlitz

Neil Armstrong

The Six-Day War

The Fall of Constantinople

www.50minutes.com

THE UNIVERSAL DECLARATION OF HUMAN RIGHTS   1

Key information

Introduction

POLITICAL, SOCIAL AND ECONOMIC CONTEXT   3

The 19th century: a changing world

The devastating effects of war

The United Nations

KEY PROTAGONISTS   10

Eleanor Roosevelt

René Cassin

A HISTORY OF HUMAN RIGHTS   15

Britain, the precursor of human rights

The time for declarations

The slow acquisition of rights

New hope: the UN and universal rights

Freedom in 30 articles: the Universal Declaration of Human Rights

IMPACT   31

The protectors of human rights

The fight continues

SUMMARY   36

TEXT OF THE UNIVERSAL DECLARATION OF HUMAN RIGHTS   39

THE UNIVERSAL DECLARATION OF HUMAN RIGHTS

KEY INFORMATION

- **When:** the night of 10 December 1948, during the 183rd session of the United Nations (UN) General Assembly.
- **Where:** Palais de Chaillot, Paris.
- **Context:** the period following the Second World War and the creation of the UN.
- **Key protagonists:**
  - Eleanor Roosevelt, First Chair of the Drafting Committee and First Lady of the United States (1884-1962).
  - René Cassin, French jurist and member of the Commission on Human Rights (1887-1976).
- **Impact:** the gradual creation of an international, regional and national judicial body with the aim of ensuring the respect of human rights and fundamental freedoms.

INTRODUCTION

On 10 December 1948, the United Nations General Assembly passed the Universal Declaration of Human Rights. This text itself, in force internationally, took on an incredible symbolic significance in a world that had just left behind the horrors of the Second World War (1939-1945). It recognised that each individual, due to the simple fact of being human, was entitled to a series of rights and fundamental freedoms that were considered inalienable and made all people equal to one another, whatever their nationality, religion, profession or ethnicity. Made up of 30 articles, the Declaration claimed to be a shield against oppression and tyranny.

The recognition of these rights took a long time and was full of pitfalls. In a world where the law often prevailed over human dignity, human rights were not guaranteed. Ignored by absolutist monarchies, stifled by colonisers and the intense search for profit, and practically annihilated by the barbarism of dictators, human rights are the result of an unremitting fight, which lasted for centuries and which has cost the lives of thousands of individuals.

It was only in the 20th century, faced with the atrocities perpetrated by totalitarian regimes, such as the planned extermination of millions of men and women in concentration camps, that the nations of the world became aware of the need to formally guarantee rights for all human beings. The UN took this mission upon itself by creating a Drafting Committee for the Universal Declaration of Human Rights in 1946. It took two years to finish this text, which granted nothing more or less than the equality of all the people in the world.

POLITICAL, SOCIAL AND ECONOMIC CONTEXT

THE 19TH CENTURY: A CHANGING WORLD

Although they had always been strived for, human rights made several major advances from the end of the 18th century. Many Enlightenment philosophers fought against dictatorial states, and the French Revolution of 1789 as well as the pronouncement of the first fundamental rights marked the peak of their fight. But the fight for the recognition of human rights was far from being over in Europe, as the continent was about to experience new inequalities in the 19th century.

After major political upsets, important changes took place in the European economy. In the space of a few decades, various countries experienced the First Industrial Revolution with the increased use of iron, coal and steam engines (1830-1870) which, as well as causing an economic boom, noticeably modified the ways in which thousands of men and women lived. These people left the countryside and came to look for work in the many factories that were being built in towns. But work did not mean prosperity for the European population which, as a consequence of economic growth, doubled in just over 50 years. In this new world, in which capitalism and profit reigned supreme, wealth was concentrated in the hands of a few people, while those who provided the heavy labour on a daily basis lived in deplorable conditions. On the other end of the scale from the upper class, a new social class was formed: the proletariat, whose demands were embodied by socialism.

In addition to these internal transformations, Europe's economic and demographic surge forced it to continually search for food resources and raw materials, which it could no longer produce itself. The necessity of these resources and the need to reach new markets to sell their products sent European nations on a new wave of colonialism and imperialism. Following various expeditions, Africa and Asia were under Europe's control. In 1884, the Berlin Conference officially ratified the new colonial borders, leaving open the possibility of a relentless exploitation of wealth and populations under the rule of European nations, with no regard for their freedom.

THE DEVASTATING EFFECTS OF WAR

As well as having a harmful impact on living conditions for the majority of the population, the incessant search for wealth ended up sowing discord among the nations. Economic and expansionist rivalries, alliances and aggravated nationalism pushed Europe to the brink of war. On 28 June 1914, the assassination of Archduke Franz Ferdinand (1863-1914), heir to the Austrian throne, in Sarajevo was the final straw. Due to the alliances between states (the Triple Alliance and the Triple Entente), this isolated incident in the Balkans plunged all of Europe into chaos.

Assassination of Archduke Franz Ferdinand.

However, in 1914, everyone believed that the war would be short-lived. This would not be the case. Stuck in a war in which no army managed to gain an advantage over another, the soldiers of the warring countries settled in for four years of trench warfare with dramatic consequences. Millions of men were turned into cannon fodder and were faced with the appearance of horrific new weapons, each one crueller than the last (such as flamethrowers and mustard gas). Within each state, as well as an economic crisis that threw ordinary citizens into poverty, public freedoms were seriously reduced out of fear of espionage. When the First World War ended on 11 November 1918, the death toll was between nine and ten million.

Faced with the cruelty of this conflict, the victors hoped that it would be the war to end all wars. However, the 1919 Treaty of Versailles and its sanctions stigmatised and humiliated the defeated Germans, who carried the seeds of an ardent desire for revenge within them. As a result of the resentment of the past, but also of the socioeconomic consequences of the 1929 crisis, extremist movements such as fascism, Nazism and Stalinism emerged. On 1 September 1939, Nazi Germany, under Adolf Hitler (Führer of the Third Reich, 1889-1945), thrust the world into another world war. As well as the horrors of war, there was an outburst of racism towards certain communities. Jews, homosexuals, the Roma and many others were accused of all that was wrong with Germany and were subjected to continuous persecution, up to and including extermination in gas chambers in concentration camps. The end of the Second World War and its atrocities, which claimed more than 40 million victims, including 6 million Jews, encouraged people to put a definitive end to conflict by establishing sustainable peace and guaranteeing human rights.

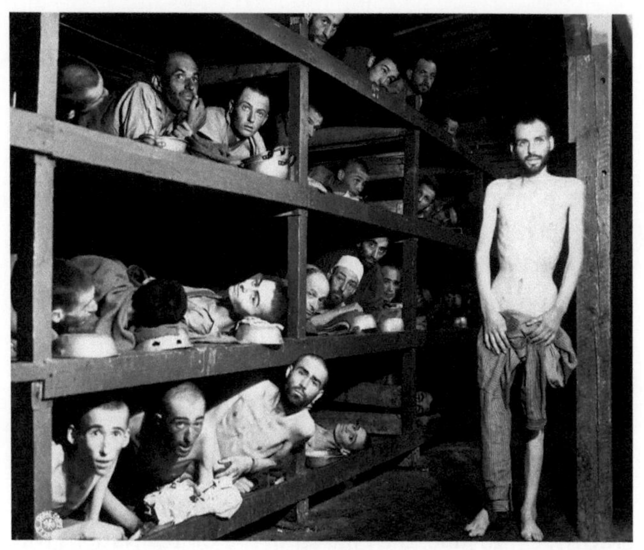

Jewish prisoners pictured at the liberation of Buchenwald concentration camp, 16 April 1945.

THE UNITED NATIONS

In the wake of the 1919 Treaty of Versailles, the victorious countries had already tried to implement an international organisation tasked with regulating relations between states and guaranteeing their collective security. The League of Nations came into force in 1920, but did not have sufficient means to intervene in the event of a conflict, meaning that it could not stop the outbreak of the Second World War. The failure of the League of Nations, however, served as a lesson to the future founders of the United Nations from 1941.

The war had not yet finished when the Allies began to think about creating a new international organisation to secure peace between countries. The first people to set out the future principles of this new cooperation were Winston Churchill (British Prime Minister, 1874-1965) and Franklin D. Roosevelt (American president, 1882-1945), in the Atlantic Charter on 14 August 1941. The project was then expanded and completed during later meetings in which the Soviet Union and China also participated (the Moscow Conference in 1943; the Dumbarton Oaks Conference in 1944; the Yalta Conference in 1945). The United Nations Conference on International Organization, which took place in San Francisco beginning on 25 April 1945, would conclude the process. On 26 June, the Charter of the United Nations was signed by 50 founding member states – joined by Poland a few days later – and came into force on 24 October, putting an end to the League of Nations, whose dissolution was made official on 31 July 1947.

Unlike the League of Nations, the UN had armed forces (the Blue Helmets) and sanctioning powers that allowed it to effectively fulfil its main object of maintaining peace. It was also made up of a General Assembly which brought together all the member states, a Security Council made up of five permanent members (the United States, the USSR, France, the United Kingdom and China) as well as ten non-permanent members, a Secretariat, an Economic and Social Council, an International Court of Justice and supple-mentary bodies such as the WHO, UNESCO and UNICEF.

Even up until now, the UN can state that it has successfully ensured comprehensive global peace. However, this is not so much the case with more regionalised conflicts where the interests of different nations have often prevented any action from the organisation, particularly during the Cold War (1945-1990) between the US and the Soviet Union. But following the Second World War, the UN's concerns were mainly centred on the recognition of the fundamental free-doms to which everyone was entitled. After several months, this work ended with new hope: the Universal Declaration of Human Rights.

KEY PROTAGONISTS

Although here we only discuss two of the significant contributors to the Universal Declaration of Human Rights, we should not forget that it was on the initiative of the whole international community. Additionally, the ideas that run through it can broadly be attributed to many philosophers and academics, such as John Locke (English philosopher, 1632-1704) and Jean-Jacques Rousseau (French philosopher, 1712-1778), and had been handed down since the Age of Enlightenment. This declaration was also theirs.

ELEANOR ROOSEVELT

Picture of Eleanor Roosevelt, dating from 1933.

Daughter of Elliot and Anne Roosevelt, Eleanor Roosevelt was born in New York on 11 October 1884. She was also the niece of Theodore Roosevelt (1858-1919), US president from 1901-1909. Her childhood was marked by the deaths of her mother in 1892 and her father two years later, leaving her an orphan at the age of just 10. Her grandmother therefore took charge of her education and sent her to a well-reputed school in London where she developed an evident interest for social causes.

When she returned to New York, she met a distant cousin, Franklin D. Roosevelt, whom she married in 1905. Much like her husband, she was active in society, and spent much of her time working for educational and social causes. During the First World War, she even entered public service by working for the Red Cross. Nonetheless, her life was completely turned upside down in 1933 when her husband became President of the United States.

Contrary to what was usually expected, Eleanor Roosevelt did not stay in her husband's shadow. As First Lady, she did not hesitate to collaborate with the president and give her opinion on important economic and international topics. She thus actively participated in the implementation of the New Deal, the interventionist policy established to counter the consequences of the crisis of 1929. She was also interested in the status of women, the fate of black citizens, relations between the US and the Soviet Union and the entry of the United States into the war in 1941.

In 1945, following the death of her husband, Eleanor Roosevelt initially thought that her public life was over.

But this was far from the truth: President Harry S. Truman (1884-1972) nominated her as United States Representative to the UN General Assembly, as well as to the Economic and Social Council. Anxious that human dignity was respected, she was naturally drawn to the chairmanship of the Commission on Human Rights from 1946 to 1951, tasked with writing a universal declaration. Presiding over work sessions and debates, the former First Lady presented the Universal Declaration of Human Rights in a plenary session at the General Assembly on 10 December 1948, considering this her life's work.

Eleanor Roosevelt then continued her work as representative to the UN until 1953. Just as she had withdrawn from public life, she was called back by President John F. Kennedy (1917-1963) in 1961 to preside over the Presidential Commission on the Status of Women. She stayed in that role for less than a year and died of cancer on 7 November 1962 in New York. Six years later, she posthumously received the United Nations Prize in the Field of Human Rights.

RENÉ CASSIN

The main drafter of the Declaration, René Cassin, was a French jurist and judge born in Bayonne to a Jewish family on 5 October 1887. After earning a law degree from the University of Aix-en-Provence in 1908, he continued his studies and became a law professor in Paris, then a barrister in 1914. When the war broke out, Cassin joined the army as a private. He was not left indifferent by the horrors of the war. Seriously wounded by machine gun fire, he would remain marked by the Great War, which led him to found the *Union Fédérale*, for former soldiers and disabled veterans.

Once the war was over, Cassin returned to his career. Notably, he taught law in several universities in France, but above all represented his country for 18 years at the League of Nations. In June 1940, confronted with the rapid advance of Hitler's troops, the jurist decided to join General Charles de Gaulle (French statesman, 1890-1970) in London and became his legal adviser, with the aim of organising the Resistance and preparing French post-war legislation.

As vice-president then president of the *Conseil d'État* from 1944 to 1960, he became actively involved in international debates by participating in the foundation of UNESCO. In 1946, he was chosen to represent France at the Commission on Human Rights and joined the Drafting Committee for the Declaration. Cassin then became a key player in the Commission's debates and wrote most of the articles of the text that was put forward in 1948. He continued his career by becoming a member of the European Court of Human Rights from 1959 to 1965, then its president from 1965 to 1968. His significant work in the field and his actions in favour of fundamental freedoms earned him the Nobel Peace Prize in 1968, thanks to which he founded the International Institute of Human Rights. The messenger of peace died on 20 February 1976, at the age of 88, in Paris and is buried at the Pantheon.

A HISTORY OF HUMAN RIGHTS

BRITAIN, THE PRECURSOR OF HUMAN RIGHTS

Human rights and the Universal Declaration of 1948 were not the result of just a handful of people at the end of the Second World War. On the contrary, their history had spanned several centuries. It is still difficult to pinpoint the origin of these freedoms, especially as the very concept of human rights is the result of a slow evolution and several opinions disagree on possible precursors: the Cyrus Cylinder, the Ten Commandments, Greco-Roman philosophy, etc.

THE CYRUS CYLINDER

The Cyrus Cylinder, discovered in 1879 during a dig on the archaeological site of Ancient Babylon, is a document written in cuneiform on a clay cylinder dated from 539 BC. It was created upon the orders of the Persian emperor, Cyrus the Great (c. 556-530 BC), following the capture of Babylon by his army. Probably hoping to win favour among the newly conquered population, he notably used it to decree the freedom of slaves and religious freedom within his empire. This document is thus considered by some people as the first written testament of human rights.

Nonetheless, it was in England in the 13th century that the first real demands appeared about freedoms that today are considered human rights. With a monarchy led by the Plantagenet dynasty, England had experienced many military failures at the end of the 12th century and the beginning of the 13th century against Philip II (1165-1223), King of France. These defeats were attributed to King John Lackland (1167-1216) and, when coupled with his financial excesses, led to a rebellion of the nobility. In June 1215, the barons, refusing to grant any financial aid to the king without recompense, successfully imposed the Magna Carta on him. This document, going against royal absolutism and laying down the bases for a parliamentary regime, signalled a major advance. One of the most important points of the Magna Carta was the implementation of a certain kind of habeas corpus, preventing the arbitrary imprisonment of a person without a trial.

Copy of the Magna Carta.

However, even though it was good that the Magna Carta existed at all, it mostly benefitted the nobility and not the rest of the population. The fight against monarchic absolutism was far from over and it would be several centuries before natural rights were recognised. It was again in England, ahead of the rest of Europe, that a body of legislative texts was created in the 17th century to guarantee the population a certain number of rights. English legislation in turn integrated the Petition of Right (1628), asserting the powers of Parliament against the king, the Habeas Corpus Act (1679), definitively reaffirming the guarantee of a legal judicial procedure for defendants, and above all the Bill of Rights (1689).

The last document was of great importance in the origins of human rights as it irreversibly put an end to the absolutism of the English monarchs. England was then in the midst of its Glorious Revolution (1688-1689). Without any bloodshed, this managed to overthrow King James II (1633-1701) and put Queen Mary II (1662-1694) and her husband King William III (1650-1702) on the throne. However, before crowning them, the Parliament wrote a declaration of rights that they imposed on future monarchs, which established its supremacy over royal power and a de facto separation of the powers. In 1689, England became a constitutional monarchy.

THE TIME FOR DECLARATIONS

Rich in its hard-earned rights, Britain nonetheless avoided granting them in its American colonies, which would have consequences. In the 18th century, the Seven Years' War

(1756-1763) gravely affected British finances, even though Britain was victorious in the war with France. The British then decided to increase their exclusive commercial rights over their colonies and raise taxes on certain products, such as stamps and tea, without consulting the settlers first. The settlers were opposed to such measures and did not miss the opportunity to invoke the Bill of Rights, particularly their right to refuse to pay any tax that had not been agreed upon by the population's representatives. But no settlements had a seat in the Parliament in London. Becoming more of a matter of principle than one relating to the economy, the slogan "No taxation without representation" quickly spread around the colonies.

Britain, for its part, refused to concede, so much so that tensions ended up descending into armed conflicts, for example with the famous Boston Tea Party in 1773. Unable to obtain the rights they wanted through diplomacy, the settlers decided to gain their independence by force. In April 1775, the American War of Independence began, ultimately ending with the creation of the United States in 1783. In the meantime, the Founding Fathers wrote a document which would be a historical milestone for human rights, the Declaration of Independence of 4 July 1776, written by Thomas Jefferson (American statesman, 1743-1826). Granting natural rights, this text, influenced by the reflections of John Locke and Enlightenment philosophy, made "life, liberty and the pursuit of happiness" central concerns in the fight against tyranny. For the first time, it also confirmed equality between individuals, the right to life and the right to an uprising in the event of oppression. In 1787, the

United States Constitution and, above all, its amendments continued to develop rights by guaranteeing religious freedom, freedom of speech, freedom of the press, freedom of assembly and the right to petition. But these texts also had their limits. Thus, the equality promised to individuals only applied to white citizens and not to other ethnicities, which were still subjected to slavery.

The Declaration of Independence, a painting by John Trumbull, 1817-1819.

Just as British rights had spread across the American continent, the ideas of the American Revolution also began to spread. Having set out to help American colonies during the War of Independence, the Marquis de Lafayette (French politician and military officer, 1757-1834) and thousands of French soldiers thus absorbed the freedoms established in America and took them back to France, then under the absolutist Ancien Régime, which had already been going downhill for several years. Catastrophic finances, debt and food shortages forced King Louis XVI (1754-1793) to summon the Estates-General on 5 May 1789 to establish a new tax. Refusing the privileged condition of the two other orders, the Third Estate, which represented 96% of the population, proclaimed itself the Constituent Assembly and promised, on 20 June, according to the principle of national sovereignty, to provide France with a constitution. The fall of absolutism was happening and, on 14 July, the Storming of the Bastille became remembered as the end of royal dictatorship.

Preparing the first French constitution, the Assembly wrote and adopted the Declaration of the Rights of Man and of the Citizen between 20 and 26 August 1789. A fundamental historical text in 17 articles, this declaration would subsequently become a good model to follow in human rights, inspiring various populations across Europe and even throughout the world. Ascribing natural and inviolable rights to each individual, the Declaration of the Rights of Man and of the Citizen put an end to privileges by instating equal rights in law, justice and taxation, but also freedoms of conscience, opinion, thought and the right to property. This proclamation of human rights, which is behind many European democracies, signalled the end of the Ancien Régime.

Declaration of the Rights of Man and of the Citizen.

THE SLOW ACQUISITION OF RIGHTS

Truly revolutionary for its time, the 1789 declaration established civil and political rights. But due to the political instability in France at the beginning of the 19th century, they would be flouted for several years, during the Terror (10 August-20 September 1792 and 5 September 1793-28 July 1794), the Napoleonic era (the Consulate of 1799-1804 and the First Empire of 1804-1815), the Restoration (1814-1815 and 1815-1830) and the Second Empire (1852-1870). The emergence of capitalism also created new inequalities, such as the exploitation of workers and child labour. The hard-earned right to vote was also far from being universal in Europe. Women, whose emancipation would take many years, were also completely subordinate to men. Finally, slavery, which was still rife in many regions of the world, and colonialism were still an insult to the principle of equality. In the face of these injustices, the 19th and early 20th centuries were the scene of a continual fight to improve human rights, particularly on a social level.

With roots in the 18th century and the social consequences of the Industrial Revolution, socialism became the engine for demands about rights in the 19th century. Its struggle for decent housing and working conditions, universal access to education and fairer distribution of wealth was even more successful after 1848 following the publication of the *Communist Manifesto* by Karl Marx (German socialist theorist and revolutionary, 1818-1883). But his ideas about class warfare and the dictatorship of the proletariat also gave rise to authoritarian countries such as the USSR (1922) and China (1949).

The 19th and 20th centuries also saw the gradual improvement of working conditions, notably with a rise in salaries and a reduction in working hours. In France, the right to strike appeared in 1864, followed by trade union rights 20 years later. Child labour was gradually regulated by age limitations (nine in Britain in 1833; eight in France in 1840, then 12 in 1874) and limits on the length of shifts. At the end of the 19th century, the development of free and compulsory schooling (in 1881-1882 in France) finally put an end to the exploitation of children in Europe. Additionally, the universal right to vote appeared at different times in different countries: 1867 for men and 1918 for women with property in Britain; 1848 for men and 1944 for women in France; 1918 for men and 1948 for women in Belgium.

In addition to these rights, the question of slavery was also central to the demands. A relic of colonisation, slavery was the one drawback of nations who advocated for equality between individuals. Abolitionist movements grew in popularity from the end of the 18th century. In Haiti, the emancipated slave Toussaint Louverture (1743-1803) led the slave rebellion which ended in the abolition of slavery in all French colonies in 1794. The Napoleonic regime, however, would reverse this progress, to the extent that it was not until 1815 that the slave trade was abolished, and 1848 that enslaved populations were definitively emancipated. Ahead of its time, Britain banned the slave trade in 1807 and emancipated its slaves in 1833. In other parts of the world, the abolition of slavery would lead to violent conflicts. This was notably the case in the United States, where the matter drove the population to civil war. Since its foundation, the United States had been divided over this issue. The northern states, progressive and undergoing industrialisation, had always been in favour of the abolition of slavery and had not thought twice about prohibiting it by law. However, the situation was very different in the South, where large export-oriented cotton farms needed a slave labour force to stay profitable. The election of the abolitionist President Abraham Lincoln (1809-1865) in 1860 was the last straw and led to the secession of 11 southern states, who joined together to form the Confederacy. From April 1861 to April 1865, the American Civil War rocked the United States and it was at the price of over 600 000 lives that freedom was finally granted to all Americans. Of course, the end of slavery did not definitively put an end to injustice. Racial segregation and colonialism would continue to wreak havoc across the world for decades to come.

NEW HOPE: THE UN AND UNIVERSAL RIGHTS

Human rights had been making progress in Europe since 1789. Their advances were nonetheless questioned twice in less than 50 years. Fierce combats between democracies and dictatorships, the two world wars destroyed the freedoms that had been acquired. This was especially the case during the Second World War, during which Nazi Germany's racist and totalitarian ideology led to the destruction of freedoms and the genocide of almost an entire population. But although the dictatorships were more powerful in the short term, democracies fared better in the long term, even if it was at the price of many lives. Following these two traumatising conflicts, mankind, having just invented the atomic bomb, became aware of the scale of its own destructive capabilities. The creation of the United Nations in the wake of the Liberation was above all a preventative measure.

A guarantor of peace, the UN claimed to be an example to follow for human rights, as its Charter demonstrated. The third paragraph laying out the aims and principles of the organisation in fact states that it aims to "achieve international co-operation in solving international problems of an economic, social, cultural, or humanitarian character, and in promoting and encouraging respect for human rights and for fundamental freedoms for all without distinction as to race, sex, language, or religion". At the time, this meant determining what was meant by "human rights" and "fundamental freedoms". However, within this organisation, which brought together countries at different stages of development and different cultures, the response was not necessarily a given. The task of defining human rights was immediately given to the UN Economic and Social Council. With the objective of drafting a new declaration of rights, the Council created the Commission on Human Rights on 16 February 1946.

Made up of representatives from 18 member states from all over the world, the Commission officially took up its post in December 1946 under the leadership of Eleanor Roosevelt. A difficult documentation task thus began, collecting together all kinds of information and recommendations on the subject of human rights with the help of other UN bodies and several NGOs, such as the International League for Human Rights. Several countries also made suggestions for the declaration, which were carefully analysed by the

Commission. On 24 March 1947, Eleanor Roosevelt finally requested the creation of the Drafting Committee, whose members were:

- Charles Dukes (1880-1948), representative of the United Kingdom
- René Cassin, representative of France
- Eleanor Roosevelt, representative of the United States and Committee Chair
- William Hodgson (1892-1958), representative of Australia
- Peng-chun Chang (1893-1957), representative of China and Vice-Chair of the Committee
- Alexander Bogomolov (1900-1969), representative of the USSR
- John Peter Humphrey (1905-1995), Director of the UN Division of Human Rights
- Charles Habib Malik (1906-1987), representative of Lebanon and Rapporteur of the Commission on Human Rights
- Hernán Santa Cruz (1906-1999), representative of Chile.

Writing the Declaration was an arduous task, to the extent that different working groups were established. René Cassin was tasked with writing many of the articles of the future declaration, which gave it an undeniably Western character. His suggestions were then analysed, revised and amended by the Drafting Committee as a whole. From January 1948, they were also sent to various governments so that each of them could give their opinion. On 18 June, the Commission finally agreed on a draft declaration.

FREEDOM IN 30 ARTICLES: THE UNIVERSAL DECLARATION OF HUMAN RIGHTS

On 10 December 1948, the project, which was named the Universal Declaration of Human Rights, was finally presented to the General Assembly during its 183rd plenary session. There were 48 votes in favour, zero against and eight who abstained from voting as they disagreed with some of the articles, without however questioning the very principle of the declaration (Byelorussia, Czechoslovakia, Poland, Saudi Arabia, Ukraine, South Africa, the USSR and Yugoslavia). This was an historic event as it was the first time a community of states had agreed upon and defined a series of rights and freedoms that were recognised as inalienable from every man, woman and child throughout the world. Additionally, the Assembly voted for additional resolutions on the right to petition, the rights of minorities and on publicising the Universal Declaration as much as possible. In memory of that day, 10 December has become Human Rights Day.

Eleanor Roosevelt presents the Universal Declaration of Human Rights.

An incredible source of inspiration for defending freedoms and fighting injustice and oppression, the Universal Declaration of Human Rights is made up of a preamble followed by a series of 30 articles defining the rights and fundamental freedoms of each individual, regardless of their nationality, gender, skin colour, religion, language or any other specification. In more ways than one, the Universal Declaration drew inspiration and elements from the 1789 declaration. It was also a smart compromise between liberal and socialist ideas.

As well as the rights obtained in the revolts and revolutions in Britain and America, the Declaration incorporated the civil and political benefits of the 1789 declaration, as well as most of the social progress of the 19th and early 20th centuries. In it, we can thus find the freedom and equality of individuals, but also their right to life; their freedom of opinion, expression, thought, religion and conscience; their right to property, legal capacity and habeas corpus; and their right to vote and stand for election, including the recognition of universal suffrage. Among the social and economic rights were the rights to work, to social protection from a trade union, to rest, to leisure, to wellbeing and to education. The free movement of people, and their right to asylum and nationality, were also present. Finally, deemed incompatible with the respect of human dignity, slavery and torture were definitively banned. The Universal Declaration was therefore the culmination of several centuries of demands for human rights. However, in 1948 this text had no legal value. It was accepted by the international community following the horrors of the war, and certainly had a significant moral impact, but it was in no way binding for the states. The fight for human rights was therefore far from over.

IMPACT

THE PROTECTORS OF HUMAN RIGHTS

As it had no legal value, the Commission on Human Rights, which observed the respect of human rights throughout the world, could in fact only give recommendations and had no sanctioning power. It subsequently continued its work to create a legal corpus and standardise human rights. In 1966, its efforts led to the conclusion of two treaties that were legally binding for the states that ratified them: the International Covenant on Civil and Political Rights and the International Covenant on Economic, Social and Cultural Rights.

Brought together in the Universal Declaration, the two main defined categories of rights were separated here. In other words, signing one of the pacts did not necessarily mean that the other one had to be signed. This division was mainly due to the context of the Cold War and the dichotomy between liberal and social ideas. For example, the right to property opposed the right to housing. Should affluent landowners be stripped of their property to give housing and land to everyone, or should everyone's property be guaranteed? Thus, while the Western Bloc signed the first treaty, the Eastern Bloc signed the second.

It would not be until 1976, however, for the two treaties to be properly enforced, after at least 35 states had ratified them. Today, they have been enforced in most of the countries of the world (168 countries for the first treaty,

163 for the second). Along with the Universal Declaration, the treaties form the International Bill of Human Rights. This legislation now has the force of law in the states that have ratified it, and they are therefore obliged to enact it. Additionally, the Commission on Human Rights (known as the United Nations Human Rights Council since 2006) now has the power to deal with human rights violations and releases a report for every country every year. Over time, the international legal corpus has grown through a series of conventions, also binding: the main ones were against racial discrimination (1966), against discrimination against women (1979), against torture and inhuman treatment (1984), for the rights of the child (1989) and for the rights of persons with disabilities (2006). The development of rights, however, is not over. New topics such as the environment or underdevelopment will undoubtedly be the next matters to be discussed.

In terms of international contributions, human rights also benefit from the protection of regional bodies. In 1950, the Council of Europe was established and the European Convention on Human Rights was written, which entered into force in 1953. Any individual who believes that their rights have been violated can thus appeal to the Convention once they have tried all of their country's internal resources. The European Court of Human Rights, established in 1959 by the Convention, is tasked with ruling in the event of litigation and human rights violation.

Finally, we must mention the major role played by the many non-governmental organisations, which have continually grown in number since the Universal Declaration. Some NGOs of course predate the Declaration, such as the Human Rights League, which was founded in 1898. They are extremely important for keeping authorities and populations alert when freedoms are not being respected. Founded in 1961, Amnesty International is one of the most emblematic examples of this duty of investigation, and writes a report each year on the state of rights and freedoms across the world.

THE FIGHT CONTINUES

Despite being legalised and protected, human rights are still constantly under threat from the barbarism and despotism of certain quarters. An example of this is the terrible civil war that took place in Rwanda in 1994, forever etched onto people's memories, which set the Tutsi and Hutu ethnicities against one another and caused the genocide of around 800 000 Rwandans, mostly Tutsis, simply because of their ethnic background. One year later, it was Europe's turn to experience to witness an unprecedented act of barbarism with the Srebrenica massacre (Bosnia-Herzegovina) of around 8000 Bosnian men, women and young people by Serbian armed forces due to their Muslim religion, with the UN's Blue Helmets looking on powerlessly.

Some countries were also the scene of discrimination and blatant infringements of freedoms despite being members of the UN, or even of the Human Rights Council in some cases. This was notably the case for Saudi Arabia, to cite one example, whose wealth of petrol allowed it to continually flout the Universal Declaration of Human Rights. The country still had slavery until 1962, and even today continues to prevent the emancipation of women by placing them under the complete authority of men and forbidding them from having the same rights – the most absurd being refusing to grant them a driving licence or freedom of movement. However, due to the economic importance of Saudi Arabia, no member state of the UN has really been able to sanction the country, much to the chagrin of many NGOs.

Finally, we cannot ignore the tragedies perpetrated by terrorist and jihadist movements in recent years. The September 11 attacks in 2001 orchestrated by Al-Qaeda, the massacres and kidnappings attributed to the terrorist group Boko Haram in Nigeria, the random executions of dozens of journalists by Daesh and the two sets of attacks carried out in Paris in 2015, the first to destroy the satirical magazine *Charlie Hebdo* and the second in various public venues including the Bataclan concert hall, were all attacks on freedom of expression, democracy, and thus human rights. This ideology is something that democracies must now compete with.

Thus, despite the achievement of international recognition of human rights and fundamental freedoms, the fight continues to ensure that these rights, which were hard fought for by millions of people, are respected. The Universal Declaration of Human Rights is certainly not perfect, but it remains a beacon, a force of hope and inspiration before the dark and cruel ways in which the world can sometimes behave, so that "[a]ll human beings are born free and equal in dignity and rights" (Universal Declaration of Human Rights, Article 1).

SUMMARY

1215
June: King John Lackland is forced to adopt the Magna Carta

1628
The Petition of Rights confirms the power of the English Parliament over the king

1679
The Habeas Corpus Act guarantees a legal trial for all defendants in England

1689
The Bill of Rights ends the absolutism of the English monarchy

1776
The United States Declaration of Independence grants natural rights to individuals

1789
French Revolution
***Aug.*: Adoption of the Declaration of the Rights of Man and of the Citizen in France**

1946
Establishment of the Commission on Human Rights

1948
***10th Dec.*: The Universal Declaration of Human Rights is adopted**

1966
Drafting of two treaties with the force of law

The Universal Declaration of Human Rights © 50MINUTES.com

- Although incomprehensive and incomplete, rights have been granted to individuals since ancient times, as the Cyrus Cylinder shows. The Cyrus cylinder is a clay cylinder, ordered by Cyrus the Great and created in 539 BC, which guaranteed religious freedom and the liberation of slaves in the Persian Empire.
- In Europe, Britain was the first place where human rights were established. In the 13th century, King John Lackland was forced to accept the Magna Carta put forward by his barons, which limited royal power and instituted a form of habeas corpus.
- The English judicial corpus, always ahead of its time, was later complemented and elaborated on by a series of texts such as the Petition of Right (1628), the Habeas Corpus Act (1679) and especially the Bill of Rights (1689), which made England a constitutional monarchy.
- These ideas were innovative for the time, but were not applied in the colonies that were under British rule, resulting in a feeling of injustice and a strong desire for freedom in the settlements. On 4 July 1776, the United States Declaration of Independence placed equality and freedom at the forefront of human rights. It was then complemented by the 1787 Constitution.
- In 1789, with the help of Enlightenment philosophy and American ideas, France underwent a revolution with the pure and simple aim of putting an end to absolutism. In August 1789, the French National Constituent Assembly gave the country a Declaration of the Rights of Man and of the Citizen, which granted natural and inalienable rights to each individual.
- From this date onwards, the 1789 declaration became

an example to follow. The fight for rights nonetheless continued in the context of the socioeconomic transformations that Europe was undergoing in the 19th century. The continuous search for freedom and equality was now combined with the slow acquisition of social and economic rights.

- The 19th and early 20th centuries thus saw the recognition of the right to work, social protection, strike action, education and much more. Child labour was limited then forbidden under a certain age. Universal suffrage was gradually obtained in democratic countries. Finally, slavery was abolished in most of the regions of the world.
- After the world wars, the international community decided to create the UN in order to maintain peace, but also to guarantee human rights and fundamental freedoms on an international scale. In 1946, the Commission on Human Rights was put in place with the objective of writing a declaration.
- After several months of arduous work, the Drafting Committee, chaired by Eleanor Roosevelt and drawing to a great extent on the work of René Cassin, wrote the Universal Declaration of Human Rights. This was put to a vote and accepted by the United Nations General Assembly on 10 December 1948.
- The Universal Declaration had no legal value, but was complemented by two international treaties and a series of conventions from 1966 onwards, with the aim of setting up a legal corpus that was binding for and respected by everyone.

TEXT OF THE UNIVERSAL DECLARATION OF HUMAN RIGHTS

PREAMBLE

Whereas recognition of the inherent dignity and of the equal and inalienable rights of all members of the human family is the foundation of freedom, justice and peace in the world,

Whereas disregard and contempt for human rights have resulted in barbarous acts which have outraged the conscience of mankind, and the advent of a world in which human beings shall enjoy freedom of speech and belief and freedom from fear and want has been proclaimed as the highest aspiration of the common people,

Whereas it is essential, if man is not to be compelled to have recourse, as a last resort, to rebellion against tyranny and oppression, that human rights should be protected by the rule of law,

Whereas it is essential to promote the development of friendly relations between nations,

Whereas the peoples of the United Nations have in the Charter reaffirmed their faith in fundamental human rights, in the dignity and worth of the human person and in the equal rights of men and women and have determined to promote social progress and better standards of life in larger freedom,

Whereas Member States have pledged themselves to achieve, in co-operation with the United Nations, the promotion of universal respect for and observance of human rights and fundamental freedoms,

Whereas a common understanding of these rights and freedoms is of the greatest importance for the full realization of this pledge,

Now, Therefore THE GENERAL ASSEMBLY proclaims THIS UNIVERSAL DECLARATION OF HUMAN RIGHTS as a common standard of achievement for all peoples and all nations, to the end that every individual and every organ of society, keeping this Declaration constantly in mind, shall strive by teaching and education to promote respect for these rights and freedoms and by progressive measures, national and international, to secure their universal and effective recognition and observance, both among the peoples of Member States themselves and among the peoples of territories under their jurisdiction.

ARTICLE 1

All human beings are born free and equal in dignity and rights. They are endowed with reason and conscience and should act towards one another in a spirit of brotherhood.

ARTICLE 2

Everyone is entitled to all the rights and freedoms set forth in this Declaration, without distinction of any kind, such as race, colour, sex, language, religion, political or other opinion, national or social origin, property, birth or other status. Furthermore, no distinction shall be made on the basis of the political, jurisdictional or international status of the country or territory to which a person belongs, whether it be independent, trust, non-self-governing or under any other limitation of sovereignty.

ARTICLE 3

Everyone has the right to life, liberty and security of person.

ARTICLE 4

No one shall be held in slavery or servitude; slavery and the slave trade shall be prohibited in all their forms.

ARTICLE 5

No one shall be subjected to torture or to cruel, inhuman or degrading treatment or punishment.

ARTICLE 6

Everyone has the right to recognition everywhere as a person before the law.

ARTICLE 7

All are equal before the law and are entitled without any discrimination to equal protection of the law. All are entitled to equal protection against any discrimination in violation of this Declaration and against any incitement to such discrimination.

ARTICLE 8

Everyone has the right to an effective remedy by the competent national tribunals for acts violating the fundamental rights granted him by the constitution or by law.

ARTICLE 9

No one shall be subjected to arbitrary arrest, detention or exile.

ARTICLE 10

Everyone is entitled in full equality to a fair and public hearing by an independent and impartial tribunal, in the determination of his rights and obligations and of any criminal charge against him.

ARTICLE 11

(1) Everyone charged with a penal offence has the right to be presumed innocent until proved guilty according to law in a public trial at which he has had all the guarantees necessary for his defence.

(2) No one shall be held guilty of any penal offence on account of any act or omission which did not constitute a penal offence, under national or international law, at the time when it was committed. Nor shall a heavier penalty be imposed than the one that was applicable at the time the

penal offence was committed.

ARTICLE 12

No one shall be subjected to arbitrary interference with his privacy, family, home or correspondence, nor to attacks upon his honour and reputation. Everyone has the right to the protection of the law against such interference or attacks.

ARTICLE 13

(1) Everyone has the right to freedom of movement and residence within the borders of each state.

(2) Everyone has the right to leave any country, including his own, and to return to his country.

ARTICLE 14

(1) Everyone has the right to seek and to enjoy in other countries asylum from persecution.

(2) This right may not be invoked in the case of prosecutions genuinely arising from non-political crimes or from acts contrary to the purposes and principles of the United Nations.

ARTICLE 15

(1) Everyone has the right to a nationality.

(2) No one shall be arbitrarily deprived of his nationality nor denied the right to change his nationality.

ARTICLE 16

(1) Men and women of full age, without any limitation due to race, nationality or religion, have the right to marry and to found a family. They are entitled to equal rights as to marriage, during marriage and at its dissolution.

(2) Marriage shall be entered into only with the free and full consent of the intending spouses.

(3) The family is the natural and fundamental group unit of society and is entitled to protection by society and the State.

ARTICLE 17

(1) Everyone has the right to own property alone as well as in association with others.

(2) No one shall be arbitrarily deprived of his property.

ARTICLE 18

Everyone has the right to freedom of thought, conscience and religion; this right includes freedom to change his religion or belief, and freedom, either alone or in community with others and in public or private, to manifest his religion or belief in teaching, practice, worship and observance.

ARTICLE 19

Everyone has the right to freedom of opinion and expression; this right includes freedom to hold opinions without interference and to seek, receive and impart information and ideas through any media and regardless of frontiers.

ARTICLE 20

(1) Everyone has the right to freedom of peaceful assembly and association.

(2) No one may be compelled to belong to an association.

ARTICLE 21

(1) Everyone has the right to take part in the government of his country, directly or through freely chosen representatives.

(2) Everyone has the right of equal access to public service in his country.

(3) The will of the people shall be the basis of the authority of government; this will shall be expressed in periodic and genuine elections which shall be by universal and equal suffrage and shall be held by secret vote or by equivalent free voting procedures.

ARTICLE 22

Everyone, as a member of society, has the right to social security and is entitled to realization, through national effort and international co-operation and in accordance with the organization and resources of each State, of the economic, social and cultural rights indispensable for his dignity and the free development of his personality.

ARTICLE 23

(1) Everyone has the right to work, to free choice of employment, to just and favourable conditions of work and to protection against unemployment.

(2) Everyone, without any discrimination, has the right to equal pay for equal work.

(3) Everyone who works has the right to just and favourable remuneration ensuring for himself and his family an existence worthy of human dignity, and supplemented, if necessary, by other means of social protection.

(4) Everyone has the right to form and to join trade unions for the protection of his interests.

ARTICLE 24

Everyone has the right to rest and leisure, including reasonable limitation of working hours and periodic holidays with pay.

ARTICLE 25

(1) Everyone has the right to a standard of living adequate for the health and well-being of himself and of his family, including food, clothing, housing and medical care and necessary social services, and the right to security in the event of unemployment, sickness, disability, widowhood, old age or other lack of livelihood in circumstances beyond his control.

(2) Motherhood and childhood are entitled to special care and assistance. All children, whether born in or out of wedlock, shall enjoy the same social protection.

ARTICLE 26

(1) Everyone has the right to education. Education shall be free, at least in the elementary and fundamental stages. Elementary education shall be compulsory. Technical and professional education shall be made generally available and higher education shall be equally accessible to all on the basis of merit.

(2) Education shall be directed to the full development of the human personality and to the strengthening of respect for human rights and fundamental freedoms. It shall promote understanding, tolerance and friendship among all nations, racial or religious groups, and shall further the activities of the United Nations for the maintenance of peace.

(3) Parents have a prior right to choose the kind of education that shall be given to their children.

ARTICLE 27

(1) Everyone has the right freely to participate in the cultural life of the community, to enjoy the arts and to share in scientific advancement and its benefits.

(2) Everyone has the right to the protection of the moral and material interests resulting from any scientific, literary or artistic production of which he is the author.

ARTICLE 28

Everyone is entitled to a social and international order in which the rights and freedoms set forth in this Declaration can be fully realized.

ARTICLE 29

(1) Everyone has duties to the community in which alone the free and full development of his personality is possible.

(2) In the exercise of his rights and freedoms, everyone shall be subject only to such limitations as are determined by law solely for the purpose of securing due recognition and respect for the rights and freedoms of others and of meeting the just requirements of morality, public order and the general welfare in a democratic society.

(3) These rights and freedoms may in no case be exercised contrary to the purposes and principles of the United Nations.

ARTICLE 30

Nothing in this Declaration may be interpreted as implying for any State, group or person any right to engage in any activity or to perform any act aimed at the destruction of any of the rights and freedoms set forth herein.

We want to hear from you!
Leave a comment on your online library
and share your favourite books on social media!

FIND OUT MORE

BIBLIOGRAPHY

- Agi, M. (1979) *René Cassin, fantassin des Droits de l'homme*. Paris: Plon.
- Bercis, P. (1993) *Guide des droits de l'homme. La conquête des libertés*. Paris: Hachette.
- Bertrand, M. (2006) *L'ONU*. Paris: La Découverte.
- Conac, G., Debene, M. and Teboul, G. (1993) *La Déclaration des droits de l'homme et du citoyen de 1789. Histoire, analyse et commentaires*. Paris: Economica.
- Halpérin, J.-L. (2005) *Histoire des droits en Europe de 1750 à nos jours*. Paris: Flammarion.
- Oberdorff, H. (2011) *Droits de l'homme et libertés fondamentales*. Paris: Librairie générale de droit et de jurisprudence.
- De Robien, B. (2000) *Les passions d'une présidente : Eleanor Roosevelt*. Paris: Perrin.
- United Nations (1948) *Universal Declaration of Human Rights*. [Online]. [Accessed 1 February 2017]. Available from: <http://www.un.org/en/universal-declaration-human-rights/>
- Verdoodt, A. (1964) *Naissance et signification de la Déclaration universelle des droits de l'homme*. Leuven: Société d'études morales, sociales et juridiques.

ADDITIONAL SOURCES

- Armitage, D. (2008) *The Declaration of Independence: A Global History*. Massachusetts: Harvard University Press.

- Hunt, L. (2007) *Inventing Human Rights: A History*. New York: W. W. Norton & Company.
- Meisler, S. (2011) *United Nations: A History*. New York: Grove Press.
- Roosevelt, E. (2014) *The Autobiography of Eleanor Roosevelt*. New York: Harper Perennial.

ICONOGRAPHIC SOURCES

- Assassination of Archduke Franz Ferdinand. © *Le Petit Journal*.
- Jewish prisoners pictured at the liberation of Buchenwald concentration camp, 16 April 1945. © H. Miller.
- Picture of Eleanor Roosevelt, dating from 1933. Royalty-free reproduction picture.
- Copy of the Magna Carta. Royalty-free reproduction picture.
- *The Declaration of Independence*, a painting by John Trumbull, 1817-1819. Royalty-free reproduction picture.
- Declaration of the Rights of Man and of the Citizen. Royalty-free reproduction picture.
- Eleanor Roosevelt presents the Universal Declaration of Human Rights. Royalty-free reproduction picture.

50MINUTES.com

History

Business

Coaching

IMPROVE YOUR GENERAL KNOWLEDGE

IN A BLINK OF AN EYE !

www.50minutes.com

© **50MINUTES.com, 2016. All rights reserved.**

www.50minutes.com

Ebook EAN: 9782806289773

Paperback EAN: 9782806289780

Legal Deposit: D/2016/12603/773

Cover: © Primento

Digital conception by Primento, the digital partner of publishers.